To our beautiful
grandchildren Isaac & Grace
Babcia & Dziadzio
2018

Adalberto Mainardi

The Star from the East

A Christmas fairy tale for adults and children

Illustrated by Martina Peluso
Translated by Sarah Seddon

Don Bosco Publications

Don Bosco Publications
Thornleigh House, Sharples Park, Bolton BL1 6PQ
United Kingdom

ISBN 978-1-909080-39-3
©Don Bosco Publications 2018
©Adalberto Mainardi

All rights reserved. No part of this publication may be reproduced, stored in a retrieval system or transmitted in any form or by any means without the prior permission in writing of Don Bosco Publications. Enquiries concerning reproduction and requests for permissions should be sent to The Manager, Don Bosco Publications, at the address above.

'La Stella venuta da Oriente: Una fiaba di Natale per grandi e per bambini'
Originally published by Elledici in Italy, 2018 (www.elledici.org)
Translated and reproduced by kind permission of Editrice Elledici, Corso Francia, 333/3–10142 Turin

Graphic Design Maison ADV, Turin

Printed in Italy by G. Canale & C. S.p.A. - Borgaro T.se (TO)

Adalberto Mainardi

The Star from the East

A Christmas fairy tale for adults and children

Illustrated by Martina Peluso
Translated by Sarah Seddon

Don Bosco Publications

Contents

Nightingale and Tulip   9

The Riddle   25

Following the Star   37

The Other Camel Train   47

*To my young friends,
and also to those
who have grown up
in the meantime.*

Adalberto
Monk of Bose

When I was a child, the time of year I was most excited about—more than my birthday, the first day of spring, and even more than the end of school—was, of course, Christmas.

On Christmas Eve I could not fall asleep unless I was told a story. The most beautiful were those of my grandfather Giovanni, whom my grandmother used to affectionately call "my Joe". As a young man, he had spent time in the desert during the war.

I still remember 'The Seven Princesses' and, of course, the story of Tulip and Princess Nightingale, the daughter of the King of Persia, the greatest of the kings of the East ...

Nightingale and Tulip

The King of Persia was the greatest of the kings of the East. At that time, after many years of wars, he had made peace with the Emperor of Rome, and the camel trains had resumed their trips to China.

One day, a camel train of Bedouins arrived in Persepolis, the ancient capital city. With them was a handsome boy with curly hair and twinkling eyes, who was good as gold. His name was Savio, but everyone called him Tulip because his cheeks were as delicate as the petals of a tulip.

He owned nothing apart from a small golden harp. His father had given it to him before he died, saying: "My son, what can I give you? I have no precious stones, neither gold nor silver, nor expensive carpets, not even weapons or camels. But I have this little harp: take it with you, it will give you courage and joy".

Tulip fought back a tear and left to seek his fortune in the world. He learnt to play the harp like an angel and would never be parted from it. On it, he created wonderful melodies (at that time, in fact, guitars were not used to compose songs).

When he reached the great square of Persepolis, Tulip gazed in wonder at the Hall of a Hundred Columns. At the centre rose a very tall white tower, surrounded by a thousand guards dressed in white; each wore a pointed white hat tipped with a gold stripe and carried a sword with a green stone on the handle.

"Who lives in the tower?" Tulip asked the merchants on the plaza.

"Do you not know?" They answered: "You must be a stranger here. Our princess lives in the tower. If you wait for sunset, you will hear her singing."

At those words, the boy decided not to leave with the camel train, but to remain in that enchanted city.

The daughter of the King of Persia was the most precious jewel in the kingdom. Her mother had named her Leila, which means 'night' in the nomadic language of the desert, because she was as beautiful as a starry night.

Her skin glowed like the moonlight, she had deep, lustrous eyes like a gazelle, and her dark hair tumbled over her shoulders in long braids. Those who saw her were entranced and lost as a sailor in the night.

Her voice was as melodious as that of a nightingale and simply perfect: not loud and strong but sensitive and poignant, like the memories of things gone by. For this, she was called 'Nightingale'.

When Leila sang in the evening, all the people of Persepolis stopped to listen to her.

When Tulip heard her sing, he was overcome by a desire to meet her. But how could he get past the thousand guards? How could he climb to the top of the tower? He did not even have an elegant outfit to wear to introduce himself to her father the King!

He remembered that he was alone in the world and became sad. He wanted to cry, but he hid behind a column to avoid being seen.

A flower seller passed by on the square: "Why are you crying, young man?" she asked.

"I would like to fly to the top of the white tower," Tulip replied, "but I have no wings."

"If you buy three tulip bulbs from me," said the florist, "I'll give you what you want."

"Oh, dear lady! I would buy all your flowers, but, alas, I have nothing to pay for them. If you want, I can play for you."

As he softly played the harp, passers-by stopped to listen. When he had finished, the florist was so moved by his music that she gave him the three bulbs for free:

"If you plant them in fertile soil and let them bathe in the dew of night and the light of the East, they will bring you happiness."

Full of hope, Tulip took the bulbs and, quick as lightning, went to plant them in a small flowerbed under the tower.

He waited for the night dew to descend and for the morning to bring the light of the East.

So, every morning and every evening he sat under the tower. People thought he was foolish; even the guards let him pass.

One evening, to ward off loneliness, Tulip took his little harp and began to play at the foot of the tower. And at that moment, carried by a light breeze, there was a distant hum, and then, more and more clearly, he could hear the words of a very sweet song.

Tulip closed his eyes as the singing gently followed the chords he played and the harmony of the song: the sheep ceased to bleat, the chirping finches, and even the wild animals, stopped to listen to them.

And the music continued until his eyes closed for sleep and the dark veil of night muffled every sound …

That night, Tulip had a magical dream.

Three pearl fishermen rose from the depths of the sea with a shell and brought it to him. He opened it and inside there was a pearl, which in his hands became a fountain of light.

Then a star with a bright tail lit up in the sky. Three flames shot from the tail and fell in a trail of fire. When they hit the ground, Tulip noticed that there were three eagles: one with golden feathers, one with purple feathers and one as black as night. They settled right where he had sown the three tulips. They stayed a while and then flew off to the highest tower of the royal palace. Then they returned, landing on the tulip-seeded flowerbed, repeating the journey several times.

The young man took courage and approached the three magnificent birds. They flew around him, grabbed his hands and feet and lifted him up into the tower.

There, he saw a girl dancing in the moonlight, swaying like the waves of the sea. She was truly the queen of beauty! But as soon as she noticed him, thin and dirty with torn clothes, the girl became very frightened.

Then Tulip opened his hands and gave her the wonderful pearl that he had received from the fishermen. The girl laughed, took his hand and led him to a garden where there were

sweet-smelling roses and dew covered the grass with pearls and emeralds, and ribbons of violets quivered in the breeze. There was a leafy palm grove in the garden, and a path so beautiful that seemed like the way to paradise.

At dawn, when the young man woke up, three tulips had blossomed in the flowerbed under the tower: one red, one yellow and one black as the night.

The Riddle

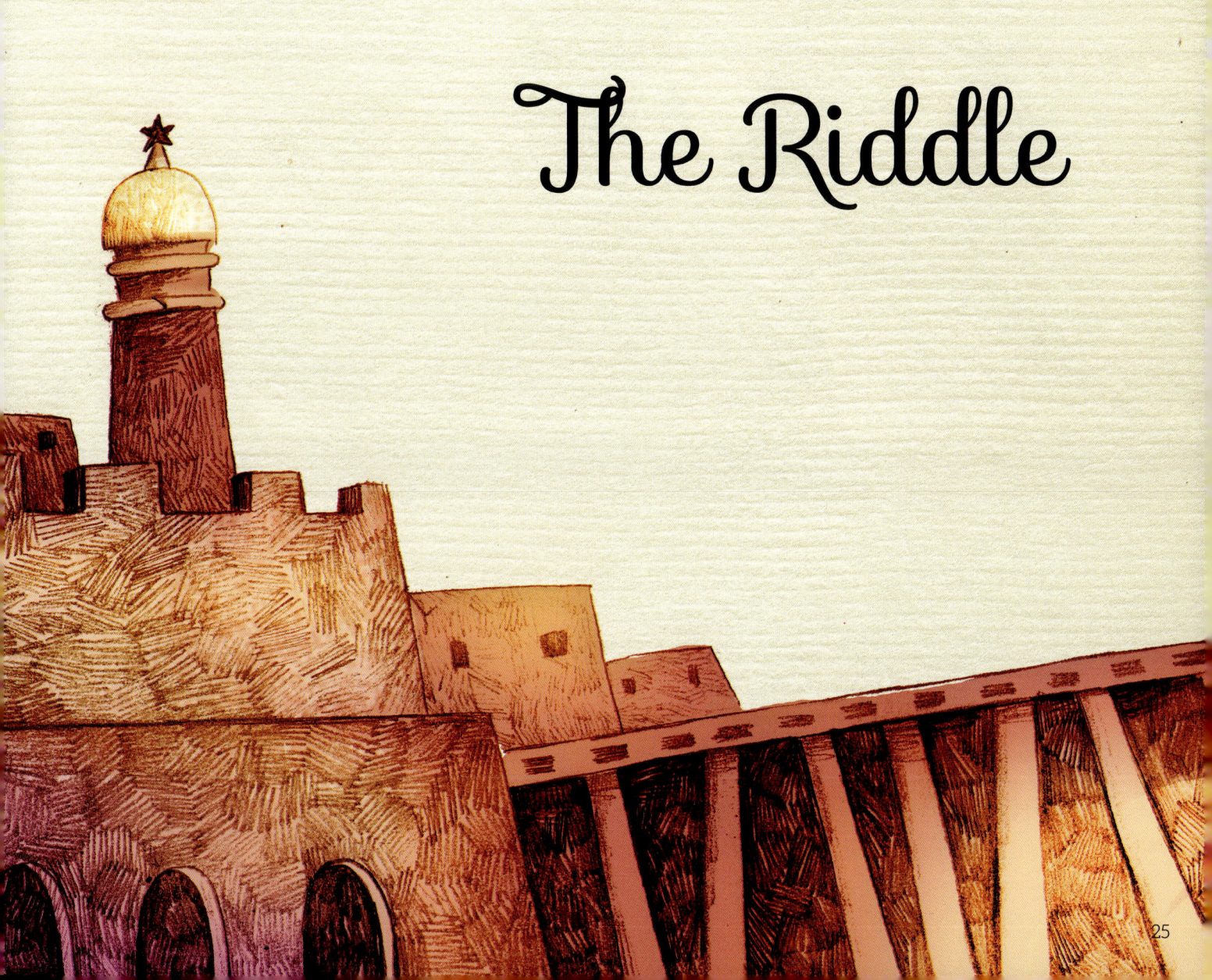

That same night, the daughter of the King of Persia also had the dream. When she awoke, she no longer wanted to eat, to sing or to dance. The once happy princess had become sad. She was sick with melancholy.

Astronomers and the greatest scholars of the kingdom were summoned.

They said that the cause of her illness was a new star that had never been seen before, which had appeared in the sky that very night.

The star had disturbed the princess's sleep: to be healed, her dream had to be interpreted.

Then the King promised to give his daughter in marriage to whoever could heal her.

Generals, princes and warriors came from all over the kingdom and even from across the sea. Tulip also presented himself at the palace.

"Who is this Bedouin who still has sand in his hair?" thought the King when he saw him: "Never mind," he said to himself, "if he makes a mistake, I'll have his head cut off!"

At that moment, the princess entered and there was a great silence: everyone was left speechless by her beauty.

And she posed her riddle:

*"On tiptoes she walks, but she is not a dancer,
All around it is dark, but she does not lose her way;
In her hair she wears a ribbon of gold;
Whether long or short, bright is her trail.
You know her at night, she leaves at dawn.
I will love only the one who solves my dream."*

"Who could it be?" everyone asked. They began to think of the most famous dancers in Persia, but none wore braids. And who appears at night and leaves in the morning? An owl, a bat? But they are not snails, they leave no trail! So, they all remained silent, because the King would behead whoever was wrong.

Even Tulip was silent, but his heart was pounding like a drum: the princess was the girl who had danced with him in his dream! He summoned his courage and asked to speak.

Seeing him so shabby, everyone else sniggered under their breath: "Now they will cut off his head!"

Tulip began playing his harp. Everyone who listened was moved, even the King. Then he started to sing softly:

*"The answer to the riddle, my beautiful queen,
Is the star, with five points and a trail:
In her night song, she shows us the way.
Admired at night, she is gone in the morning:
A treasure that guides us, but is not stolen."*

As soon as he had finished, the princess clapped her hands with joy. She recognised the harp that had accompanied her nocturnal song: she had danced with that handsome boy in the secret garden in her dream. Tulip had healed her!

In accordance with the King's promise, the wedding should have been celebrated; but the King had no desire to give his daughter to that poor, skinny stranger who did not even have a bed to sleep on.

The King's cup-bearer whispered to the King: "All the princes have brought a gift for your daughter: precious stones, gold, silver, fine fabrics and even camels. But what has this beggar given her? He cannot marry the daughter of the King of Persia!"

He only said that because he was wicked and wanted to marry the princess himself.

"Quite right," thought the King, and he asked Tulip, "What gift do you bring worthy of the Queen of Persia?"

Tulip remembered his dream:

"I will bring the pearl of a thousand reflections, which in the hands of the beholder becomes a fountain of light."

"Bring me this pearl," Nightingale whispered,

"and I will be your bride."

The King did not know what to say, as it seemed they were in agreement. "I'll make it harder for him," he thought. He gave him a year, six months and one day to bring the pearl. "In a few months," the King reasoned to himself, "this Bedouin will surely lose, and my daughter will forget him."

Tulip was not discouraged, and he took his

harp and left. The King's cup-bearer, full of envy, followed him secretly on the dusty road, and when the boy fell asleep under a wall, he dropped some lime on his eyes to blind him. "Now he can no longer find the marvellous pearl," thought the evil cup-bearer.

When he awoke, Tulip could no longer see the stars, the sun or the moon. He had become blind.

A year passed, six months passed, but the pearl of a thousand reflections promised by Tulip did not appear in Persepolis. The King's cup-bearer rubbed his hands and said to the King: "Long live the King! That little Bedouin made fun of us. I said that he was an impostor. In truth, no one is worthier than me to marry your daughter."

And so, he convinced the King to let him marry the princess instead.

But Nightingale wanted to wait until the last night for Tulip's return.

She climbed to the top of the tower and stared at the stars. They all seemed to be trembling because her eyes were full of tears. But one star shone more brightly than the others and reflected in her tears, while the wind carried them away like a trail of light.

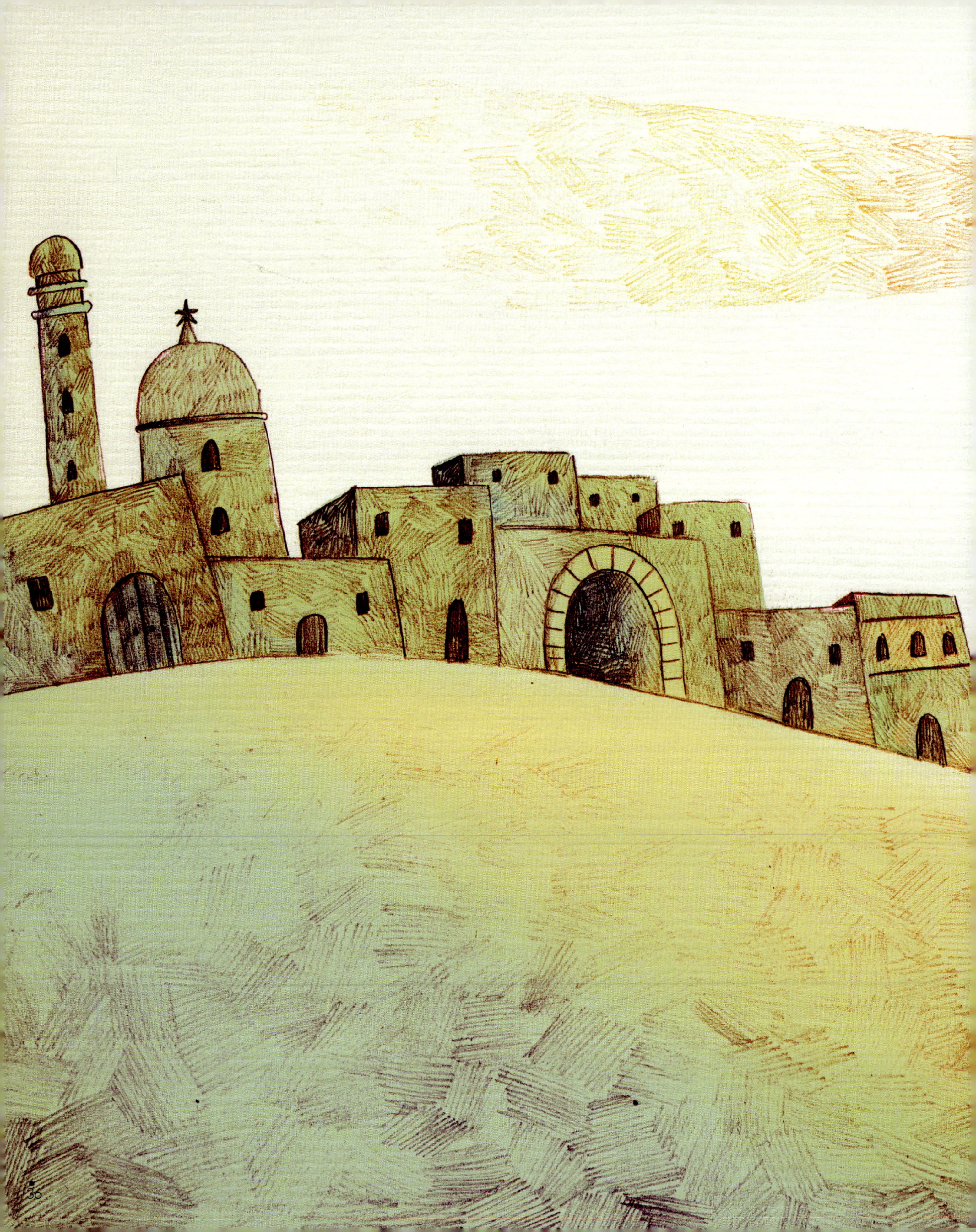

Following the Star

When he realised they could not see each other again, Tulip thought he would never find the pearl of a thousand reflections, nor return to Persepolis and see Nightingale's smile again. He lost hope.

Just then he heard a voice behind him that he recognised: "Hey, young man, why are you standing there doing nothing at the side of the road?"

It was the old woman who sold tulips.

He told her about his misfortunes.

"Do not despair, my friend," said the old woman. "Come with me, I have to go to the western ports. You can keep me company, and by playing in the streets, you will attract people who will buy my flowers. And maybe your lucky star will guide you to the wonderful pearl."

And so, they went from city to city, selling flowers on the streets, and the sound of Tulip playing his harp enticed buyers. Even the passing swallows copied his music and sang it along the Silk Road.

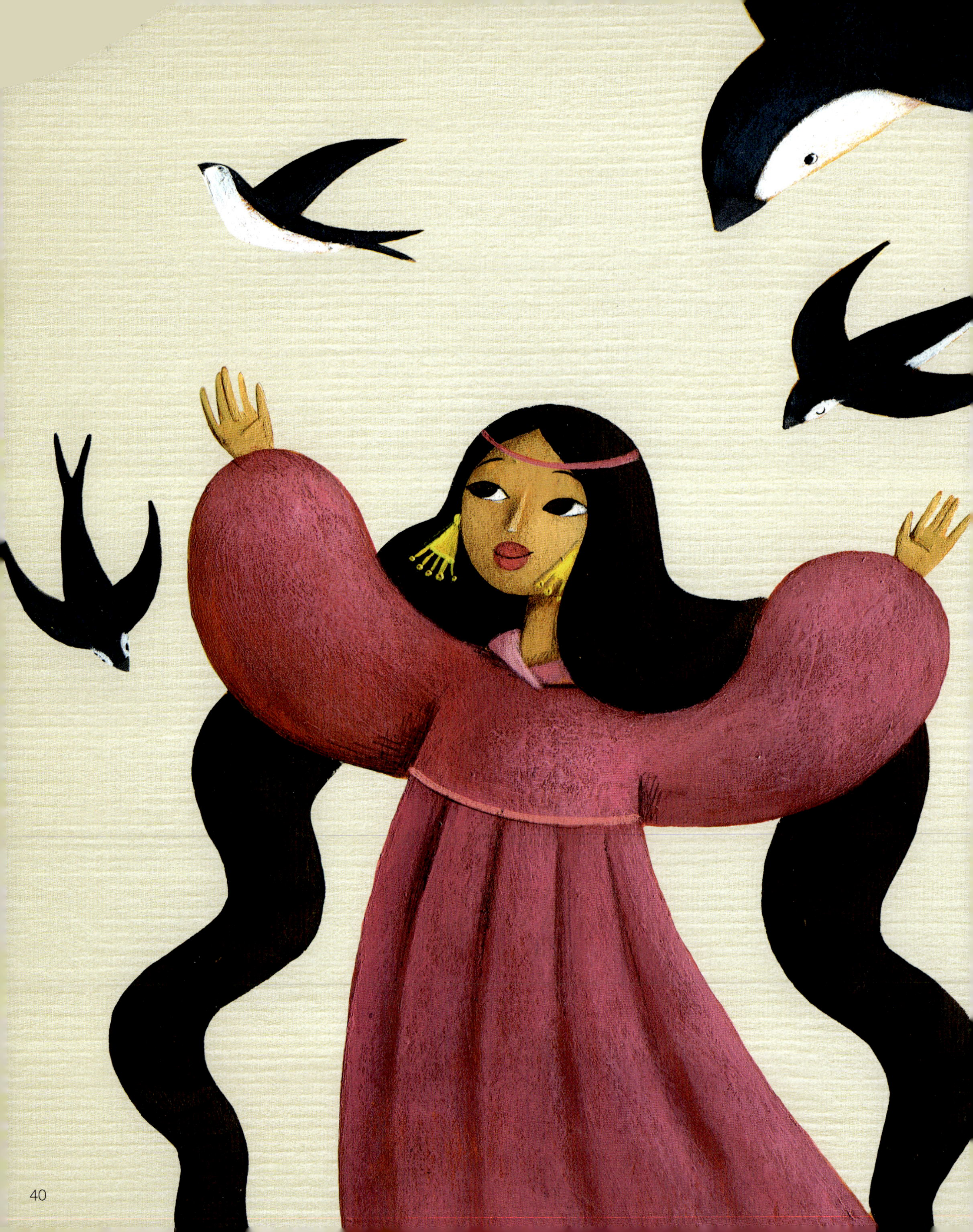

At the top of the tower, Nightingale was crying. Alas, the dawn was about to break, and Tulip had not returned. But there appeared a dark speck on the horizon, growing larger until it wrapped the tower: it was a flock of swallows. Flying around the princess, they made a great noise, as if they were speaking. But Nightingale, of course, knew the language of birds: the swallows told her that Tulip was alive, that he had not forgotten her!

The princess immediately decided to search for him and devised a bold plan. She let it be known in the court that she was not well and that she would not leave her room for two days. Left alone, she cut her long, flowing hair and disguised herself as a Bedouin. No one would recognise her.

Then she took the hair that she had cut off, put it in a basin of water and hummed folk songs: one for strength, one of stretching and (for safety) one of flotation: the hair dramatically grew longer. Plaiting the hair, she made a rope, thin but resistant, and in the middle of the night she climbed down from the window.

At the first light of day, a guard saw her in the courtyard and shouted, "Hey you! What are you doing here? Do not you know that you cannot stay in this place?"

And he threw her out through the big door. It was just what she wanted! From that moment she was no longer Princess Leila.

At the market, she learned that a camel train was looking for someone to do the most basic jobs: cleaning the camels, preparing food, washing clothes.

She went to the camel train leader and persuaded him to let her work. He took her with him, convinced that she was a boy looking for adventures in distant countries.

And so, before anyone noticed her disappearance, Princess Leila was already far away. Soon, she became so good and quick with her work that everyone started to like her. They called her Eli.

"Hey there, boy, come here, lay the table and prepare some food," one of them said.

"Hey there, boy, come with me today to do the laundry," another said.

So, Eli spent almost two years working in the camel train.

One evening she was very tired and wanted to cry: she thought she would never find her friend Tulip. She looked up at the sky and saw a star with a bright trail. Then she wiped away her tears, sighed and fell asleep.

That night, Eli dreamt about a vast expanse of desert, then a river and mountains; in the distance a city of gold shone with its golden walls and golden roofs.

In the city there was singing and dancing, and the people were happy. The hills were covered with olive trees and when the wind touched them, the leaves rustled. On the city shone a

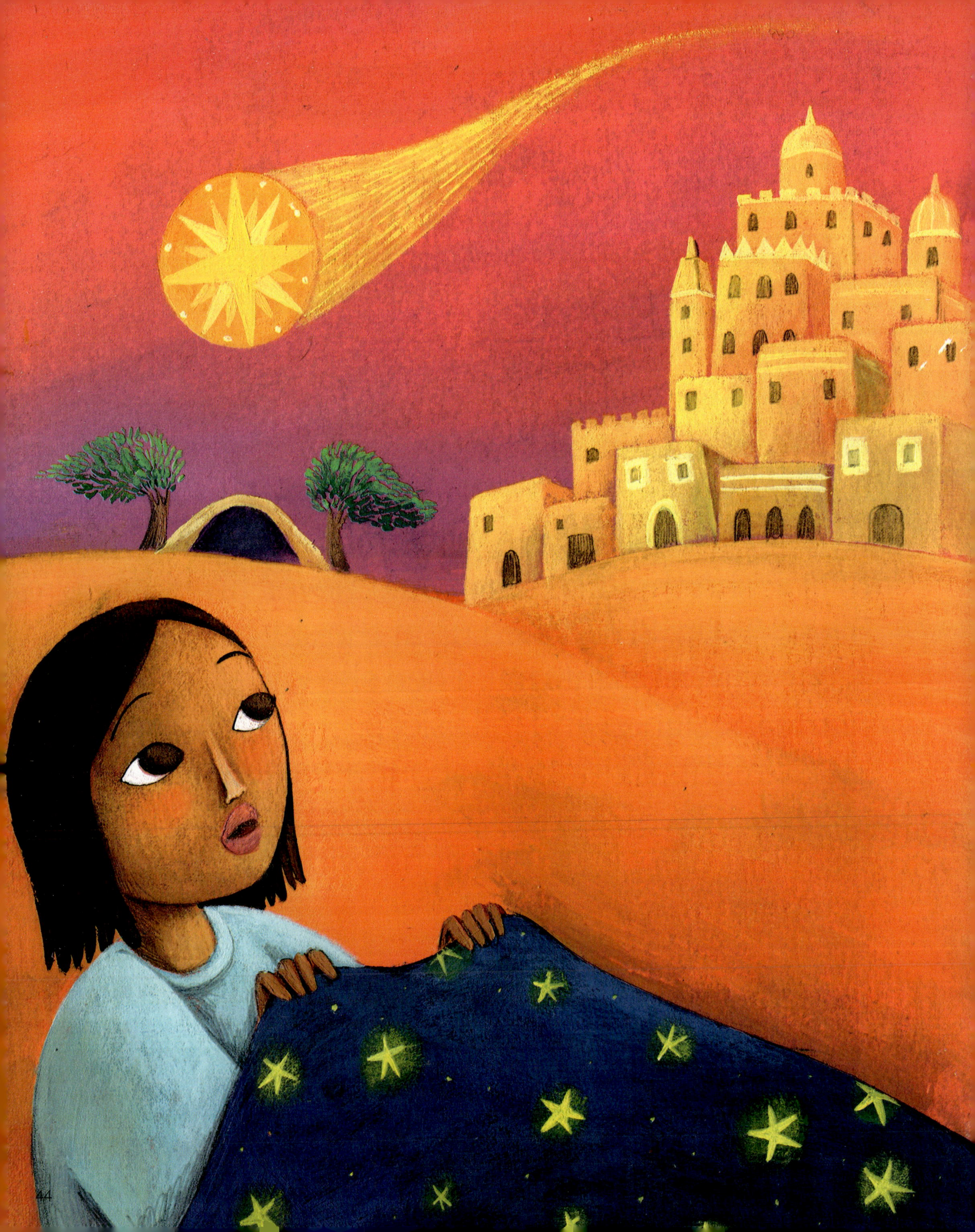

marvellous star which had settled nearby above a cave.

The next evening, everyone gathered around the fire to listen to stories. Eli recounted her dream. Then the camel train leader exclaimed:

"Of course, this is the Golden City, the City of Peace!"

On hearing those words, Eli grew hopeful. The next morning, she went to ask how much she was owed because she wanted to leave. The camel train leader gave her the agreed pay, but he guessed her heart's desire:

"My little friend, where do you want to go? It is dangerous to venture alone in the desert … If you want to reach the Golden City, I suggest you wait. In a few days we will pass by it."

At dawn on the third day they saw the golden roofs of the City of Peace shine. The camel train leader called Eli, hugged her and let her go:

"A star shines as you leave," he said.

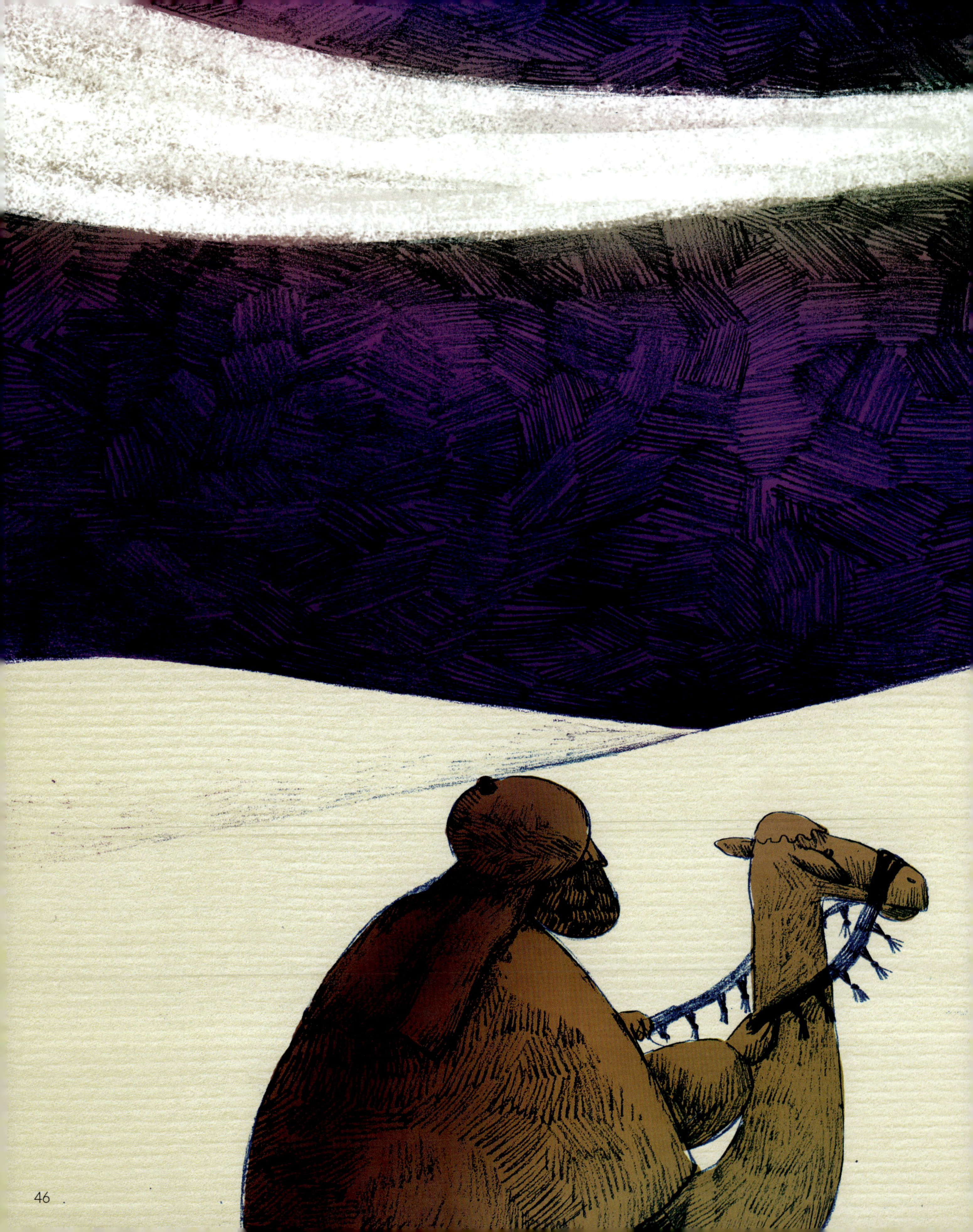

The Other Camel Train

The palace of the King of Persia, without Nightingale's singing, became silent and sad. No one wanted to work, nor the soldiers to go to war, nor the chefs to cook.

One day a very strange camel train arrived in the city. Everyone talked about it. It carried no silk, no spices, no carpets. Three learned and wise men led it: one dressed in purple, one in gold and one in black. Their names are recorded in the chronicles of the kingdom of Persia: Màlgalat, Gàlgalat and Saràthin. They wanted to talk to the King.

"Long live the King!" they said.

*"We are three Eastern travellers,
In peace with gifts we have come
Over field and fountain, moor and mountain
Following a star.
We have come to you to request,
Your astronomers to question:
There are no others on the whole earth
Who know the path of the star."*

The King summoned the head of his astronomers. For three days and three nights the wise men of the kingdom analysed the signs in the sky and the scrolls in the library. On the third day, the head of the astronomers gave a response.

"Long live the King!" he said, "The star that these three men follow is the same star that appeared two years ago: from the East it is going to the West. Princess Leila, who saw it in a dream, most certainly fled to follow it. It signifies the birth of a Great King, who will bring peace to all the people of the earth and to you too."

The King then gave the three travellers gold, precious perfumes and rare ointments:

"Go, follow the star. But I pray you, along the way, look for my daughter, whom I have lost, and I cannot find peace any more!"

Then the three left, heartened and full of hope.

After many months of travel, Màlgalat, Gàlgalat and Saràthin stopped in a city because they had not seen the star for a month. In the market square they heard very sweet music. Next to a florist, a young boy accompanied a poignant song on his harp:

"Who will restore my sight?
Only the queen of beauty
Only the queen of beauty
Only the queen of beauty."

The old florist said, "O wise men, buy my flowers and you will find your star again."

The three travellers were stunned, but they were even more surprised when the boy asked:

"Please, take me with you."

"That star in the East
That appeared on the world,
Though I cannot see it,
I sing about it in the dark."

The three men then took him with them. Together they travelled through known roads and unknown tracks, wide streets and narrow lanes, escaping from marauders and robbers, meeting good people and bad people.

Every evening, among the first stars there was one brighter than the others, with a long trail. When they saw it, the men rejoiced; even Tulip, hearing about it, was comforted in his heart.

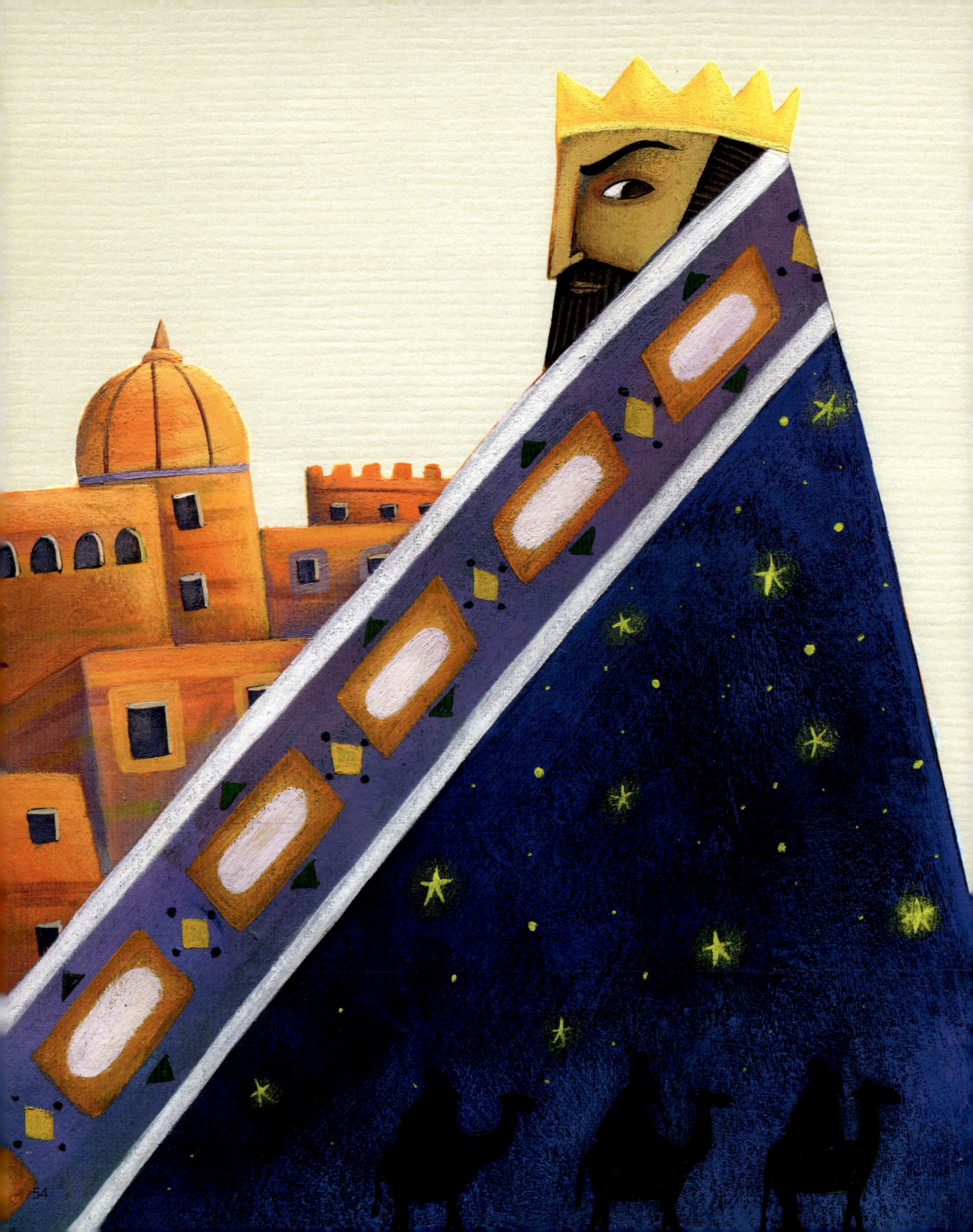

Guided by the star, the three travellers arrived at the Golden City and stood before the king. Despite his splendour, this king had a false and bad heart. They asked him where the King of Peace was to be born, signified by the star. The king questioned the scribes of the city. They answered:

"It is written that he will be born in a village not far from here, which certainly cannot be the smallest of the towns of this country, because from it the Great King will come."

Then the three men resumed their journey with confidence. The star guided them. When they saw it resting above a cave, their hearts filled with joy. They entered with the gifts they had brought: gold, frankincense and myrrh.

The servants stood outside to warm themselves around the fire. Many people came from all over. There was also a boy from one of the camel trains who tried to enter the cave but could not.

Then the boy took off his turban, and—oh wonder! The 'boy' was a beautiful girl: her long black hair fell over her shoulders. All who saw her let her pass.

Oh yes, it was our Nightingale! Her hair that she had cut had grown back long. After leaving the camel train to follow the star, she had reached the cave. On entering, she saw a child sleeping in the arms of an incredibly young and beautiful woman.

"Mary, look!" the man next to her said, pointing to the princess.

The woman turned, smiled sweetly and gave her the little one to hold. As soon as the newborn left his mother's embrace, he burst into tears. At that moment, from a dark corner drifted the melody of a gentle lullaby, and little-by-little the enchantment of the music captivated everyone, and the child stopped crying. But Nightingale's heart leapt because she had recognised the sound of Tulip's harp.

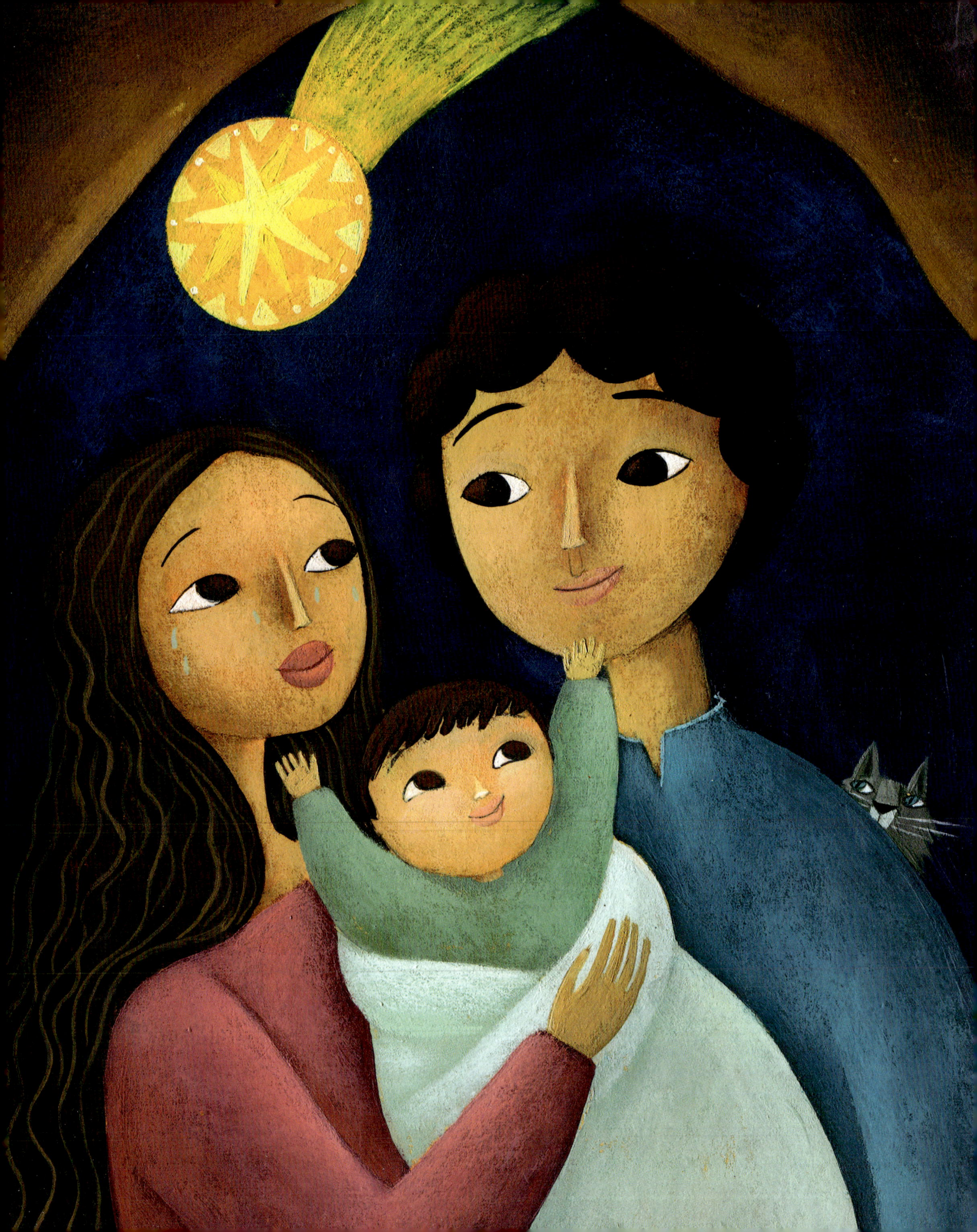

She turned and saw him there, softly playing in the shadows.

Tulip had carefully crept along the wall in order not to fall, and hearing the baby cry, he had pulled out his harp and had begun to play.

Nightingale quietly approached him without making a sound; she still held the baby in her arms and, when Tulip had finished playing, she put the little boy close to the kind face of the young man. The baby grabbed Tulip's nose, and then his ears, and put his little hands in his eyes, kicking as newborn babies do. Then Tulip raised his head and saw the child laughing, and behind him he saw beautiful Nightingale weeping, and he, too, began to cry and laugh.

His eyes were opened! Tulip could see again! He had found his marvellous pearl, the beautiful Nightingale!

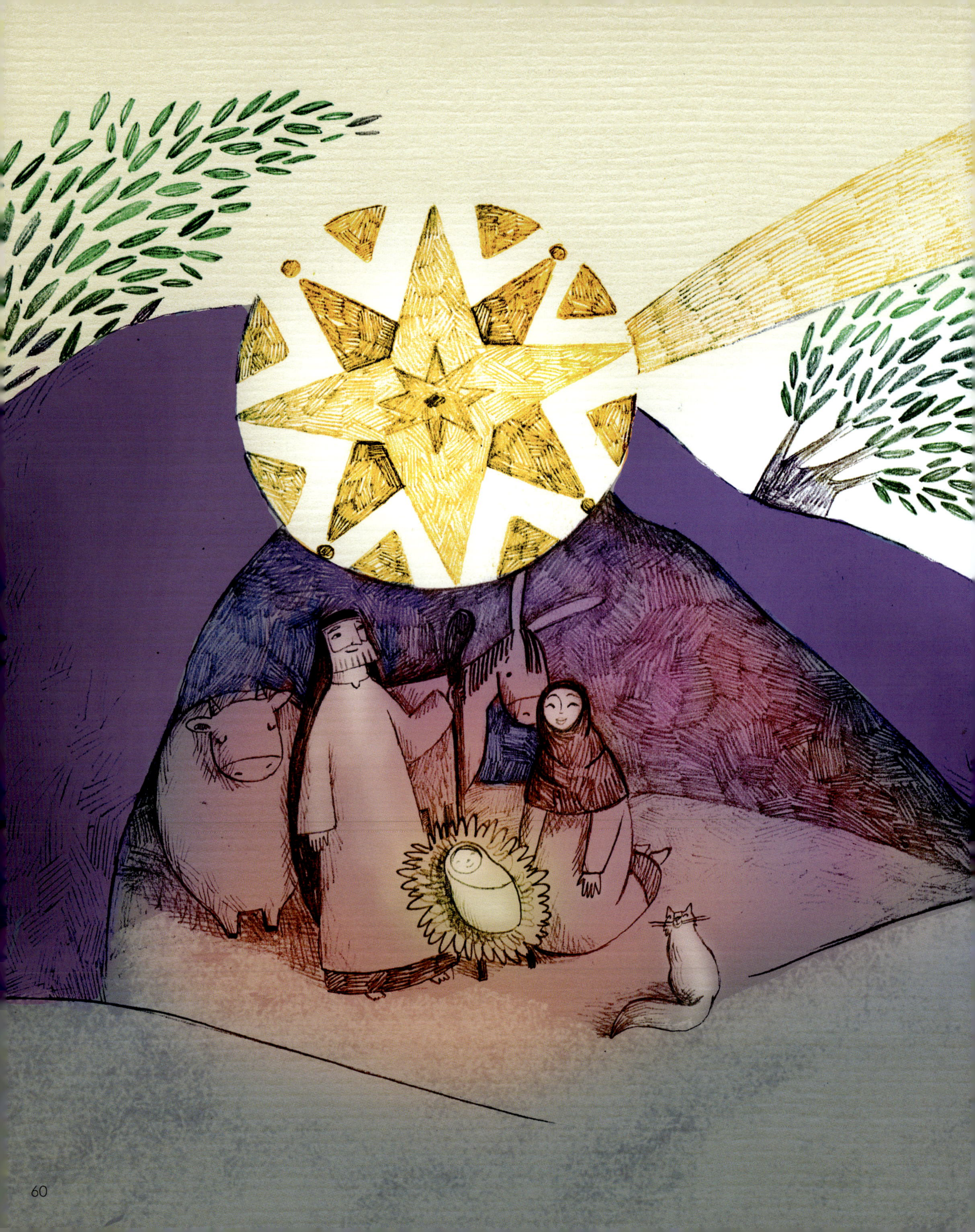

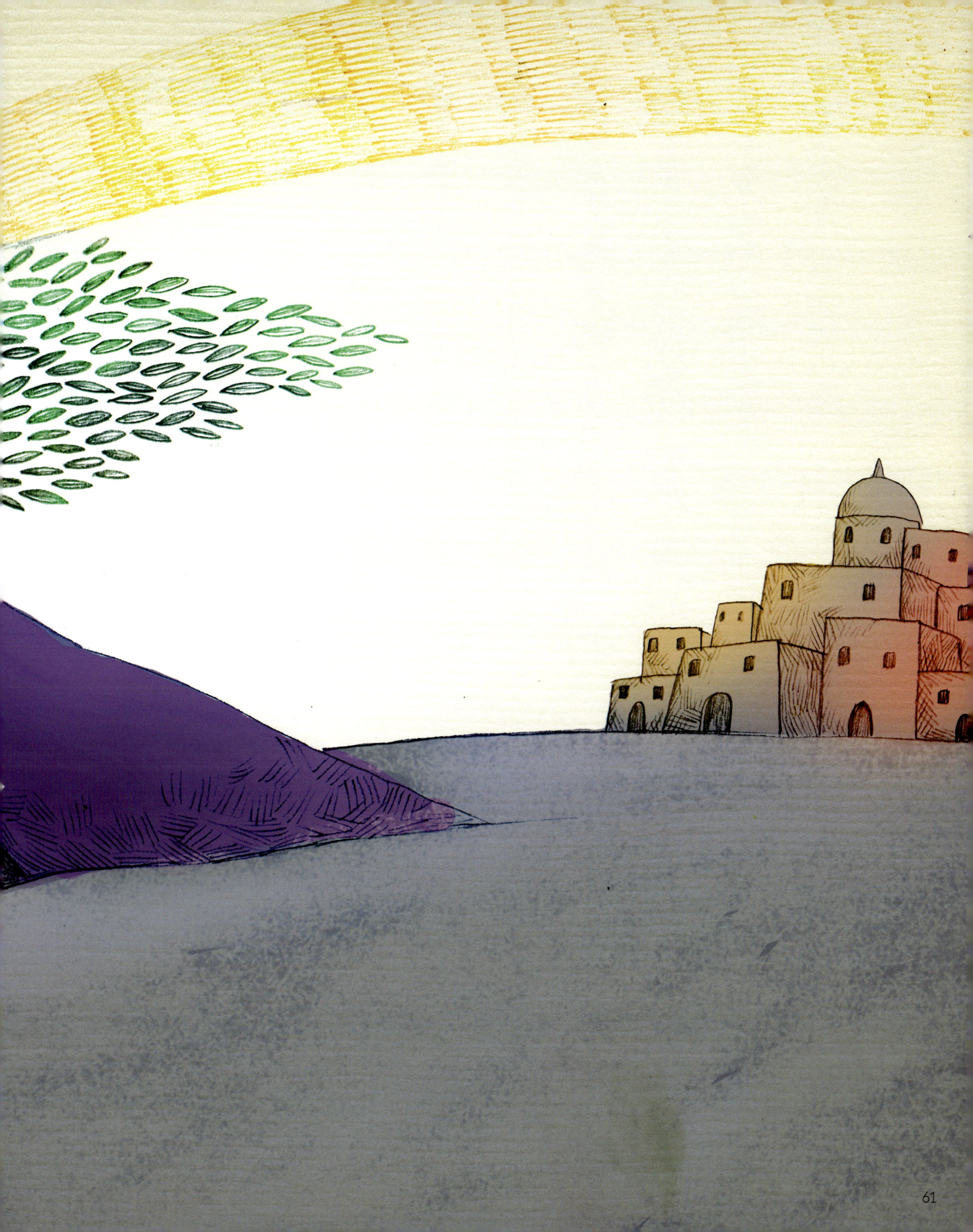

At this point I had always fallen asleep, so my story ends here.

What happened next, I read in history books: Nightingale and Tulip returned to Persia and married, and while they lived there was peace along all the borders of the kingdom. I later learnt that the Golden City is Jerusalem, the City of Peace, and in our part of the world, we call the three wise travellers Melchior, Caspar and Balthazar: the Three Kings.

63

This really is the story that my grandfather Giovanni told me, who had heard it from a silk salesman, who picked it up from a pearl merchant who had heard it in full from a Persian cat ...